DEATH OF A PARTY ANIMAL

Doonesbury books by G. B. Trudeau

Still a Few Bugs in the System
The President Is a Lot Smarter Than You Think
But This War Had Such Promise
Call Me When You Find America
Guilty, Guilty, Guilty!
"What Do We Have for the Witnesses, Johnnie?"
Dare To Be Great, Ms. Caucus
Wouldn't a Gremlin Have Been More Sensible?
"Speaking of Inalienable Rights, Amy…"
You're Never Too Old for Nuts and Berries
An Especially Tricky People
As the Kid Goes for Broke
Stalking the Perfect Tan
"Any Grooming Hints for Your Fans, Rollie?"
But the Pension Fund Was Just Sitting There
We're Not Out of the Woods Yet
A Tad Overweight, but Violet Eyes to Die For
And That's My Final Offer!
He's Never Heard of You, Either
In Search of Reagan's Brain
Ask for May, Settle for June
Unfortunately, She Was Also Wired for Sound
The Wreck of the "Rusty Nail"
You Give Great Meeting, Sid
Doonesbury: A Musical Comedy
Check Your Egos at the Door
That's *Doctor* Sinatra, You Little Bimbo!

In Large Format

The Doonesbury Chronicles
Doonesbury's Greatest Hits
The People's Doonesbury
Doonesbury Dossier: The Reagan Years

A DOONESBURY BOOK BY
G.B. Trudeau

DEATH OF A PARTY ANIMAL

AN OWL BOOK · HENRY HOLT AND COMPANY · NEW YORK

Published by Henry Holt and Company, Inc.,
521 Fifth Avenue, New York, New York 10175.
Distributed in Canada by Fitzhenry & Whiteside Limited,
195 Allstate Parkway, Markham,
Ontario L3R 4T8.

Library of Congress Catalog Card Number: 86-81209
ISBN 0-8050-0073-9 (pbk.)

First Edition

Printed in the United States of America

The cartoons in this book have appeared in newspapers
in the United States and abroad under the auspices of
Universal Press Syndicate.

1 3 5 7 9 10 8 6 4 2

ISBN 0-8050-0073-9

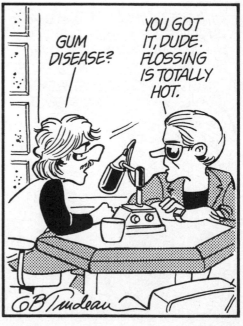

DR. DAN, WHAT ABOUT THAT NOTORIOUS BABY BOOM SUBSPECIES— THE YUPPIE? IS HE A PHENOMENON OF THE PAST?

WELL, AS AN OBJECT OF MEDIA INTEREST, THERE'S NO QUESTION HE'S IN REMISSION.

THE YUPPIE'S VERY RESILIENT, THOUGH. I HAVE NO DOUBT HE'LL BE BACK, PROBABLY IN TIME FOR THE CHRISTMAS SEASON. HE TENDS TO RE-APPEAR IN CYCLES.

HE SOUNDS LIKE A FRUIT FLY.

HE'S BEEN CALLED WORSE.

GB Trudeau

YOU SEE, MARK, A TRULY COHESIVE GENERATION ONLY COMES ALONG ONCE OR TWICE A CENTURY. THAT'S WHY THE BOOMERS WILL BE TRACKED FOR THE REST OF THEIR LIVES.

THIS GENERATION IS LIKE A GREAT COMET, BLAZING THROUGH THE FIRMAMENT, CARRYING WITH IT A DREAM AS BOUNDLESS AS THE UNIVERSE ITSELF!

WHEW..

HOW WILL WE KNOW WHEN IT'S OVER?

"ESQUIRE" WILL RUN A PIECE ON THE HOT NEW FUNERAL HOMES.

GB Trudeau

LARRY, DO YOU THINK THE TWO DAYS IN GENEVA WILL BE ENOUGH TIME FOR REAGAN TO CONDUCT SERIOUS ARMS NE-GOTIATIONS?

WELL, AS YOU KNOW, THE PRESIDENT'S PRECONDITION TO SERIOUS TALKS IS AN END TO SOVIET INVOLVEMENT IN AFGHANISTAN, ETHIOPIA, NICARAGUA, ANGOLA AND CAMBODIA.

WE'RE ALSO PUTTING HUMAN RIGHTS AND INDIVIDUAL FREEDOM ON THE TABLE. BASICALLY, WE'RE ASKING THE SOVIETS TO RENOUNCE THEIR WHOLE WAY OF LIFE.

SO YOU'RE EXPECTING A PRETTY QUICK ANSWER?

FRANKLY, WE'RE LOOK-ING FOR WAYS TO KILL TIME.

I ASKED MY DADDY WHAT THIS "STAR WARS" STUFF IS ALL ABOUT.

HE SAID RIGHT NOW WE CAN'T PRO-TECT OURSELVES FROM NUCLEAR WEA-PONS, AND THAT'S WHY THE PRESIDENT WANTS TO BUILD A PEACE SHIELD. IT'D STOP MISSILES IN OUTER SPACE..

.. SO THEY COULDN'T HIT OUR HOUSE. THEN NOBODY COULD WIN A WAR. AND IF NOBODY COULD WIN A WAR, THERE'S NO REASON TO START ONE. MY DADDY'S SMART.

OOPS, ONE GOT THROUGH. 'BYE.

DADDY SAYS THE PEACE SHIELD OVER OUR HOUSE IS ACTUALLY HUNDREDS OF LITTLE PEACE MACHINES.

THE PEACE MACHINES ARE THOUSANDS OF TIMES MORE COMPLICATED THAN ANY WEAPONS EVER BUILT.

BUT DADDY SAYS WITH ENOUGH TIME AND MONEY, THE PENTAGON CAN BUILD MOST ANYTHING.

THIS IS THE SGT. YORK.

HI, THIS IS MARK SLACKMEYER, BROADCASTING LIVE FROM LAFAYETTE PARK. ALL THIS WEEK, WE'LL BE TALKING TO THE HOMELESS ON A SPECIAL SHOW CALLED "URBAN HOME COMPANION."

URBAN HOME COMPANION

IN A MOMENT, WE'LL MEET MY FIRST GUEST, MS. ALICE SCHWARTZMAN, A FORMER GARMENT WORKER AND LONG-TIME HABITUÉ OF THE PARK..

URBAN HOME COMPANION

BUT FIRST, SOME BACKGROUND. THIS WINTER, THE NUMBER OF HOMELESS HERE MAY SURPASS THAT REACHED DURING THE DEPRESSION..

HA, HA, HA, HA! YUK!

URBAN HOME COMPANION

ALICE, THAT ISN'T FUNNY.

OOPS. SORRY. I THOUGHT YOU WERE DOING AN OPENING MONOLOGUE.

URBAN HOME COMPANION

THAT'LL HAVE TO BE THE LAST QUESTION, BOYS! I HAVE TO GET BACK AND HIT THE BOOKS!

SO SAID LOTTERY WINNER ZONKER HARRIS THIS MORNING AS HE RETURNED TO CLASSES HERE AT THE ACADEMICALLY GRUELING BABY DOC COLLEGE OF PHYSICIANS.

$23 MILLION JUST DOESN'T SEEM TO HAVE CHANGED THIS UNAFFECTED YOUNG MAN AND HIS BOYHOOD DREAM OF BECOMING A DOCTOR.

YO, BABE! I'LL GIVE YOU TEN GRAND TO TAKE MY BIO-CHEM EXAM!

OKAY.

GB Trudeau

THANKS FOR CHECK-
ING, MIKE, BUT WHAT
CAN I TELL YOU? YOUR
ALMA MATER IS STILL
THE ARMPIT OF THE
UNIVERSE.

WHAT
ABOUT
YOUR
ROOM-
MATE?

TRIPPY
THE
TRIP?

HE CONTINUES TO FLAME
INCANDESCENTLY ACROSS
THE SKIES. JUST WHEN
YOU THINK HE'S REACHED
NEW HEIGHTS OF EAGER-
BEAVER WEENIE-DOM..

HI HO!
GUESS
WHAT I
JOINED!

.. HE
TOPS
HIMSELF.

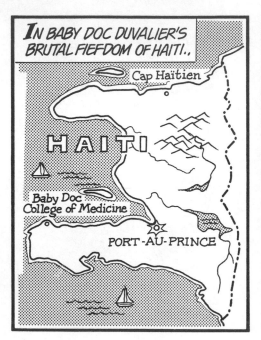

CARRIED ALONG BY GENTLE TRADE WINDS OFF HAITI..

..A SOLITARY FLY..

..BEGINS HIS DAY.

BZZZZZ!

SIR? SIR?

GBTrudeau

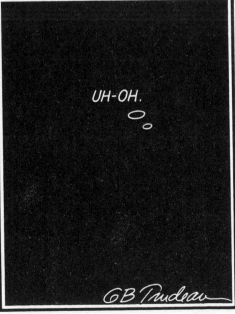

GB Trudeau

DEAR GOD,
'FORE HE DIED, PAPPY USTA SAY,
"DARLIN', HARLINGEN, TEXAS, DON'T
MATTER NOWAYS TO NOBODY!"

'COURSE, THAT WAS 'FORE THE COUNTY
PAVED ROUTE '77. AND NOW MR.
REAGAN SAYS HARLINGEN'S ONLY
TWO DAYS' DRIVE FROM MANAGUA!

I'M SCARED, GOD.

AN ABC NEWS CLOSE-UP

The
Color
Red

©BTrudeau

"Dear God!"

THE COLOR RED. A LOT OF FOLKS HAVE BEEN SEEING IT LATELY, ESPECIALLY THOSE LIVING IN A DUSTY LITTLE TOWN AT THE SOUTHERN TIP OF TEXAS.

HERE IN HARLINGEN, THE SANDINISTAS ARE TAKEN VERY SERIOUSLY. WHEN PAT BUCHANAN PREDICTED THE FIRST STRIKE WOULD COME AT SAN DIEGO, FOLKS HERE HOOTED UP A STORM!

BIP!

AS ONE OLD-TIMER PUT IT, "SAN DIEGO, MY BUTT!" AND THAT'S A PRETTY TYPICAL REACTION HERE IN THE TOWN THAT'S JUST.. **TWO DAYS' DRIVING TIME FROM MANAGUA!**

IT'S QUIET OUT THERE. **TOO** QUIET.

DEAR LORD, LET THEM MISS THE CUT-OFF AT JEB'S PLACE..

DOWN AT THE BLACK CAT CAFE, I ASKED THE BOYS IF THEY'RE READY TO MIX IT UP WITH THE SANDINISTAS.

READY? DAMN **STRAIGHT** WE'RE READY! BEEN READY EVER SINCE THE PRESIDENT DECLARED A NATIONAL EMERGENCY TO MEET THE NICARAGUAN THREAT!

UH.. WE'RE IN A NATIONAL EMERGENCY?

YUP. WHERE YOU BEEN, MAN? REAGAN ANNOUNCED IT LAST MAY! THIS IS DAY 334 OF THE CRISIS!

BUT YOU'RE ALL SO.. SO RELAXED!

HEE, HEE!

THAT'S WHAT WE **WANT** 'EM TO THINK!